MARY EMMERLING'S
AMERICAN COUNTRY
HEARTS

STAR ON A METAL DOORMAT.

MARY EMMERLING'S
AMERICAN COUNTRY
HEARTS

PHOTOGRAPHS BY CHRIS MEAD

DESIGNED BY JOE CHAPMAN

Clarkson N. Potter, Inc. / Publishers
DISTRIBUTED BY CROWN PUBLISHERS, INC., NEW YORK

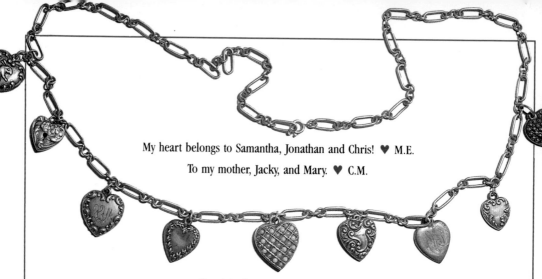

My heart belongs to Samantha, Jonathan and Chris! ♥ M.E.

To my mother, Jacky, and Mary. ♥ C.M.

Published by Clarkson N. Potter, Inc., 225 Park Avenue South, New York, New York 10003 and distributed by Crown Publishers, Inc., New York

CLARKSON N. POTTER, POTTER, and colophon are trademarks of Clarkson N. Potter, Inc.
Manufactured in Japan

Library of Congress Cataloging-in-Publication Data
Emmerling, Mary Ellisor.
[American country hearts]
Mary Emmerling's American country hearts / photographs by Chris Mead.
p.   cm.
1. Handicraft.   2. Heart in art.   I. Mead, Chris, 1959–
II. Title.   III. Title: American country hearts.
TT157.E45   1988   88-6506
745.5—dc19   CIP
ISBN 0-517-56989-2
10   9   8   7   6   5   4

What is it that draws us to the heart motif? Why does the sight of a valentine warm us and make us feel loved? Among family and friends, my passion for hearts and heart-shaped things is notorious. The first time I received a gift of a heart was when my grandmother gave me a charm bracelet filled with silver hearts. Each time those charms clinked together I thought of my grandmother and felt loved. When I grew older and discovered my love of antiques and American folk art, my collection of hearts really started to grow. I remember how it began: my mother and I were shopping on the eastern shore of Maryland and I saw a wooden candle paddle with a heart-shaped handle. I had to have it. Ever since, I've felt a special affinity for almost any heart-shaped object, especially country antiques embellished with hearts. As I travel across the country, my eye is automatically drawn to heart-shaped things: cutting boards, turquoise Indian bracelets, kitchen utensils, samplers, quilts, picture frames, kerosene lamps, candy molds, belts adorned with silver hearts, antique Indian beaded bags, wooden boxes—even a big heart melted in the middle of a pool after a snowstorm in the country. Once my eye learned to spot them, I knew that there would always be a heart wherever I looked. That very first gift of a heart from my grandmother gave me a sense of what it felt like to receive—and give—a heart and that has stayed with me to this day. Whenever I find a special heart card, valentine, candy, or trinket, I buy it and give it to someone special. I have a friend who sends me heart-shaped crackers all the way from California, which makes *me* feel special, and my collection of hearts has grown to include many that I've been given as gifts over the years. That's the great thing about hearts—everyone loves them. They reflect not only romantic love, but also the love between family and friends. So to all of you, I'll return a heart—an American Country heart—from my heart to yours.

Thanks,

Mary Emmerling

Famed in song and story, depicted on valentines and stitched into heirloom quilts, the simple yet appealing shape of a heart has been with us for thousands of years. Over the centuries, it has evolved from a symbol of power to an expression of love and friendship. ♥ Twenty thousand years ago, when Cro-Magnon man painted a heart on the wall of his cave it represented a goal: if he could capture the heart of a powerful enemy, then that power would become his. To the ancient Greeks and Egyptians, the soul resided in the heart, directing all actions, both corporeal and spiritual. ♥ It was not until the Middle Ages that the emblem of the heart came to represent love and romance. With Christianity on the rise throughout Europe, hearts began to appear in illuminated manuscripts and in religious manuscripts and paintings, symbolizing man's love for God. Later, the heart came to express an idealized kind of love between man and woman. Hearts were embroidered, appliquéd, and woven onto court costumes and armor, further secularizing the heart motif. ♥ It was not long after this that the heart was incorporated into the rituals of romance. An English tradition, dating from the 17th century, was the giving of a pair of gloves embellished with a heart, usually accompanied by the verse: "If that from Glove you take the letter G/Then Glove is love and that I send to thee." This heart-and-hand love token was often given as a marriage proposal; if the lady accepted she wore the gloves to church Easter Sunday. ♥ Another English custom that became popular in New England during the 18th century was the sometimes delightful, sometimes disappointing tradition of pronouncing the first boy a girl saw on St. Valentine's morning her valentine. Equally unnerving was the custom of picking valentines by lot at a dance or party on St. Valentine's Eve—though there is reason

 to believe that special arrangements could be made with the organizers of the event if one wanted to give fate a hand. ♥ Courting couples were not the only ones to make use of the universally appealing heart motif. During the 18th and 19th centuries, the heart was used as a symbol for trade and professional associations in both Europe and America. In England during the early 18th century, for example, a heart-shaped sign hanging outside an establishment signified the premises of a marriage broker. A group of 18th-century New York City fire fighters called themselves the "Heart and Hand Company" and decorated their uniforms and firebuckets with hearts. ♥ Although artists in both England and Germany are credited with using the heart in a more modern context, it is in American folk art that the heart motif truly came into its own. Drawing on the tradition of the Pennsylvania German Fraktur artists,

among others, 18th-century colonists decorated even the simplest household items with hearts. Everything from cheese molds to hatboxes had hearts chip-carved, painted, or chiseled onto them. Often, these were tokens of affection from members of the household to the women of the house. In return, colonial women embellished the things they made out of necessity—quilts, linens, samplers—with hearts, flowers, and other decorations that expressed their caring. ♥ Itinerant artists, sometimes known as "Heart and Hand Artists" owing to their tendency to sign their work with a heart and hand, made home furnishings adorned with elaborate designs that often included hearts. For example, the "Sunflower" or "Hadley" chests of the Connecticut River Valley were covered with hearts, flowers, leaves, pinwheels, and tulips. "Heart and Crown" chairs, also from Connecticut, were named for their not uncommon motif, which had its roots in the Christian tradition. ♥ *The giving of heart-shaped keepsakes was not reserved for Valentine's Day until the 1850s. Until then, they were given year-round as tokens of love and friendship. These heart-shaped love letters or mementos might have been drawn with pen and ink, painted with watercolors, cut with scissors, outlined with pinpricks, or carved on a whale's tooth by a lovesick sailor during his years at sea. No matter what form they took, the giving of these valentines, so reminiscent of the courting customs practiced in England and Germany, simply evolved into the annual holiday we now call Valentine's Day.* ♥ *With the advent of the Industrial Revolution in America, it became possible to mass-produce hearts on Valentine's Day cards, furniture, clothing, or whatever else was popular. Those handmade love tokens—a cast-iron skillet with a heart forged into its handle,*

Love Unites Us

family genealogies decorated with hearts by itinerant artists, a gift made by one person out of love or admiration for another— could not be mass-produced and today have all but died away.  *However, these one-of-a-kind expressions of feeling still exist in the collections of heart lovers who have either inherited them or sought them out in antiques shops and flea markets. And there are still ways to bring a sense of the warmth and caring a heart symbolizes into our lives; we may not be able to carve a Heart and Crown chair, but we can bake a batch of heart-shaped muffins for a loved one's breakfast, make our own cut-out valentines, stitch a heart-shaped patchwork quilt, or weave together fragrant strands of dried herbs to create a heart-shaped wreath. And they will be just as special— perhaps even more—as those that are a century old because they have been made with love.*

T

he mother's heart is the child's schoolroom.

HENRY WARD BEECHER

PAINTED MINIATURE DOLL'S CRADLE WITH HEART CUT-OUTS. PENNSYLVANIA. C. 1890.
RIGHT: DOLL'S CRADLE WITH CUT-OUT HEART. PENNSYLVANIA. C. 1850.

FRAMED MOURNING PICTURE. NEW ENGLAND. LATE 18TH CENTURY.
RIGHT: POTTERY INKWELL WITH HEART DECORATION. PENNSYLVANIA. C. 1850.

U nlearned, he knew no schoolmate's subtle art,
No language, but the language of the heart.

ALEXANDER POPE

*T*he heart of the fool is in his mouth, but the mouth of the wise man is in his heart.

BENJAMIN FRANKLIN

We cannot kindle when we will
The fire that in the heart resides,
The spirit bloweth and is still,
In mystery our soul abides.

MATTHEW ARNOLD

TIN LANTERNS. DELAWARE. C. 1880.
RIGHT: HANGING IRON CANDLE SCONCE. VERMONT.

JOKER WEATHERVANE WITH HEART TAIL. CONNECTICUT. C. 1830.

M

y heart leaps up when I behold
A rainbow in the sky.

WILLIAM WORDSWORTH

M_y

secrets cry aloud.
I have no need for tongue.
My heart keeps open house,
My doors are widely flung.

THEODORE ROETHKE

PAINTED HANGING CUPBOARD. PENNSYLVANIA. C. 1880.
RIGHT: DOWER CHEST WITH PAINTED HEARTS. PENNSYLVANIA. C. 1820.

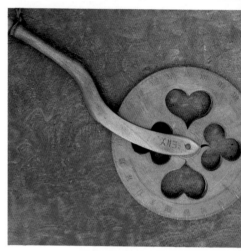

MOLD FOR STAMPING BUTTER. PENNSYLVANIA. C. 1800.

REDWARE PLATE. EARLY 19TH CENTURY.

TIN NUTMEG GRATER. NEW YORK. 19TH CENTURY.   YELLOWWARE KITCHEN BOWL WITH HEARTS. NEW ENGLAND.

H

*e that is of a merry heart
hath a continual feast.*

PROVERBS 15:15

LATE-1800S HEART-HANDLED BREAD BOARD.
CONNECTICUT.

OPEN CUPBOARD WITH PAINTED HEART. PENNSYLVANIA. C. 1840.

FIVE HEART WAFFLE IRON. PENNSYLVANIA. C. 1800–1850.

IVORY JAGGING WHEEL OR PIE CRIMPER.
NANTUCKET. C. 1850.

CHARLESTOWN STONEWARE JUG WITH THREE HEARTS.
WEST VIRGINIA. C. 1880.

The head is stately, calm, and wise
And bears a princely part;
And down below in secret lies
The warm, impulsive heart.

JOHN GODFREY SAXE

HEART KEY LATCH ON A CONNECTICUT PAINTED BLUE BOX.
RIGHT: PATCHWORK QUILT. 1840–1850. Photo courtesy of the Brooklyn Museum.

When
*the voices of children
are heard on the green
And laughing is heard on the hill,
My heart is at rest within my breast
And everything else is still.*

WILLIAM BLAKE

ABOVE: **WALNUT CHAIR WITH HEART CUT-OUT. NEW ENGLAND. C. 1860.**

Where
we love is home,
Home that our feet
may leave,
but not our hearts.
OLIVER WENDELL HOLMES

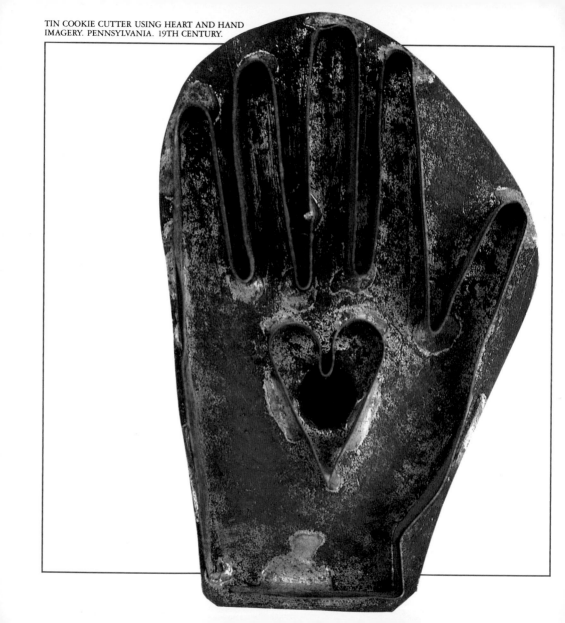

A heart for an old friend,
A hand for the new:
Love can to earth lend
Heaven's hue—

JAMES STEPHENS

T*he*
Queen of Hearts
She made some tarts,
All on a summer's day;
The Knave of Hearts
He stole the tarts,
And took them clean away.

ANONYMOUS

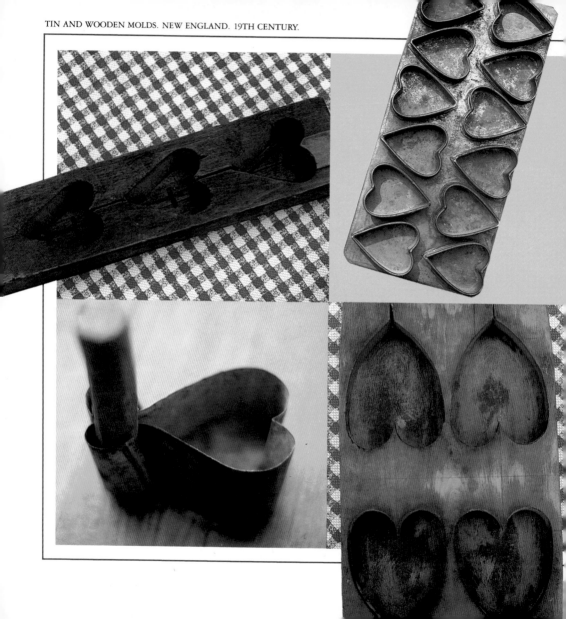

The way to a man's heart is through his stomach.

FANNY FERN

HOOKED HEARTH RUGS.
LATE 19TH CENTURY.

TOASTING FORKS, SPOONS, SPATULA, HOOK. WOOD AND IRON. NEW ENGLAND. 18TH CENTURY.

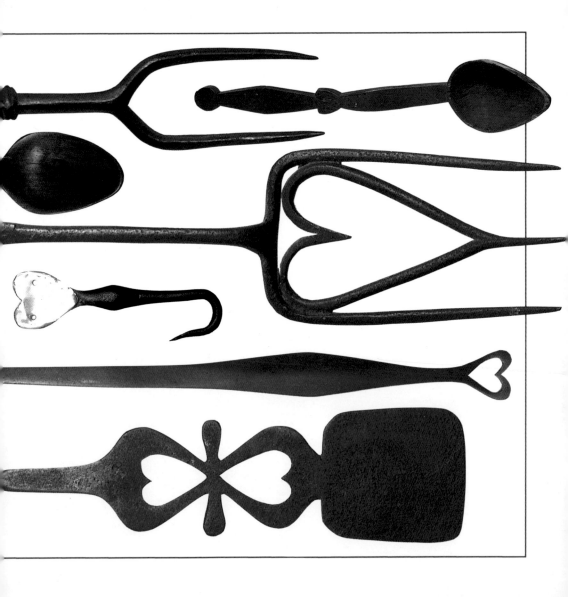

TIN FIRE CARRIER WITH WOOD HANDLE AND EMBOSSED HEART DESIGN. EARLY 19TH CENTURY.

L

*et us, then,
be up and doing,
With a heart for any fate;
Still achieving, still pursuing,
Learn to labor and to wait.*

HENRY WADSWORTH LONGFELLOW

HEART-SHAPED PINE TABLE. CONNECTICUT. LATE 19TH CENTURY.
RIGHT: A VERMONT COW NAMED MARY.

K
eep
*a green tree in your heart
and perhaps the singing bird will come.*

CHINESE PROVERB

TOP: GARDEN HOE. EARLY 19TH CENTURY.
WOODEN CHILD'S SWING SEAT. NEW ENGLAND. EARLY 19TH CENTURY.

TWIG TABLE WITH HEART-SHAPED DESIGN. VIRGINIA. LATE 19TH CENTURY.

APPLIQUÉD ANCHOR-AND-HEART QUILT PIECE. VERMONT. C. 1880.
RIGHT: HEART-SHAPED "SAILOR'S VALENTINE." MASSACHUSETTS. C. 1830.

*D*istance
ly lends enchantment,
rough the ocean waves divide;
sence makes the heart grow fonder,
nging to be near your side.

ARTHUR GILLESPIE

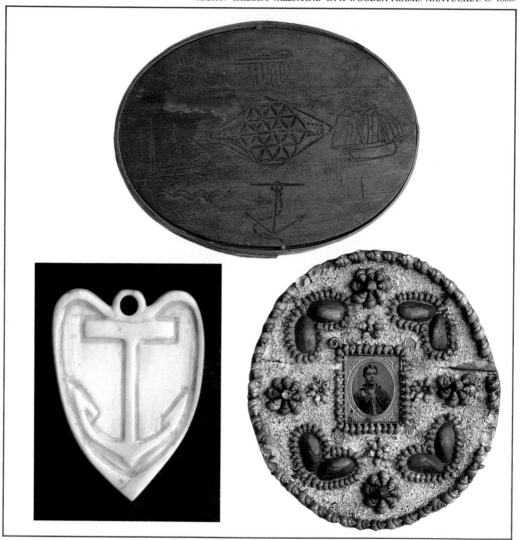

CLOCKWISE FROM TOP: SAILOR'S DITTY BOX WITH HIGHLY CARVED TOP; A ROUND "SAILOR'S VALENTINE"; A SAILOR'S IVORY LOVE TOKEN. NANTUCKET. MID-19TH CENTURY.

*Futile the winds
To a heart in port.*
EMILY DICKINSON

W

hen
I was one-and-twenty
I heard a wise man say,
"Give crowns and pounds and guineas
But not your heart away."

When I was one-and-twenty
I heard him say again,
"The heart out of the bosom
Was never given in vain;

'Tis paid with sighs aplenty
And sold for endless rue."
And I am two-and-twenty,
And Oh, 'tis true, 'tis true.

A. E. HOUSMAN

TRAMP ART MIRRORS AND BOX. PENNSYLVANIA. C. 1875–1900.

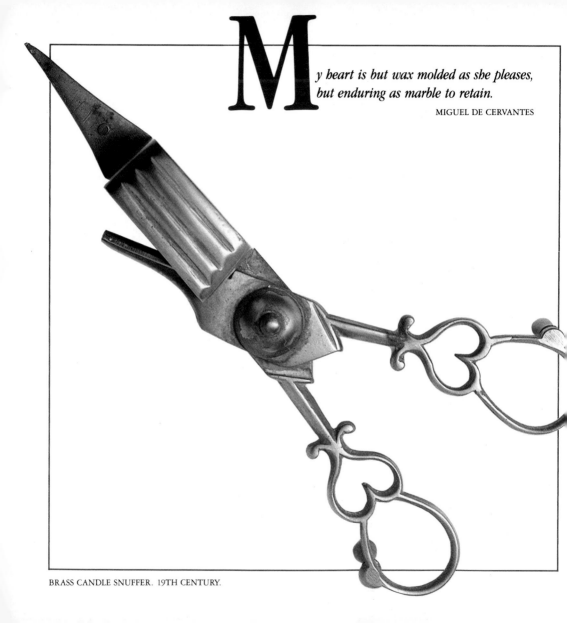

My heart is but wax molded as she pleases,
but enduring as marble to retain.

MIGUEL DE CERVANTES

BRASS CANDLE SNUFFER. 19TH CENTURY.

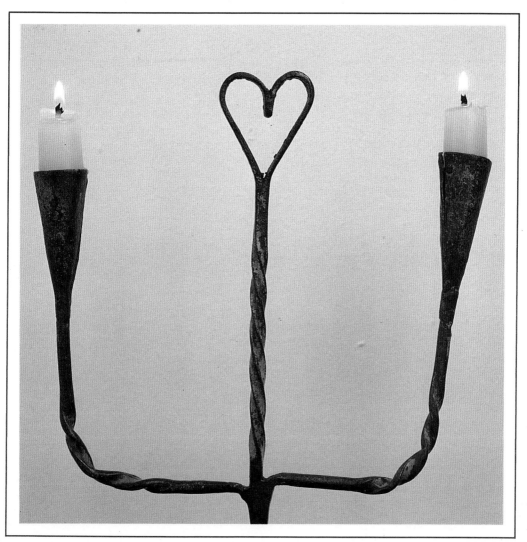

NEW ENGLAND IRON CANDLE HOLDER WITH HEART HANDLE.

LOVE POCKET ORIGINALLY FOLDED TO ENCLOSE A LOVE TOKEN.
UNFOLDED, EACH SIDE REVEALS A MESSAGE OR POEM. PENNSYLVANIA. C. 1880.

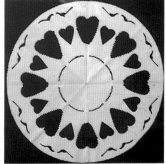

I

f you want to know yourself, Just look how others do it; If you want to understand others, Look into your own heart.

J. C. VON SCHILLER

ABOVE: FRAMED HEART AND HAND VALENTINE. MASSACHUSETTS. LATE 18TH CENTURY.
ABOVE RIGHT: CUT-OUT VALENTINE. PENNSYLVANIA. 1790.

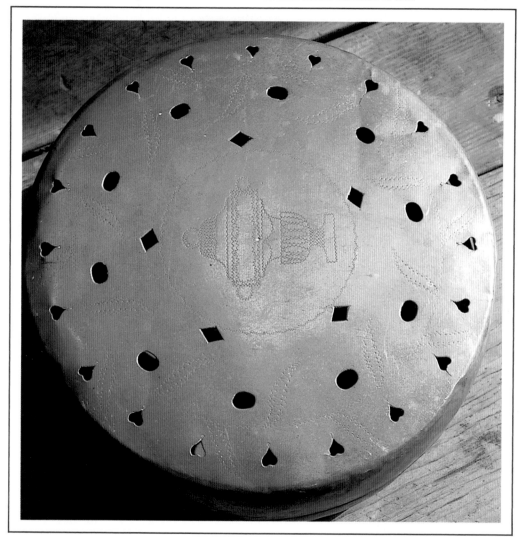

BRASS BED WARMER. NEW ENGLAND. C. 1830.

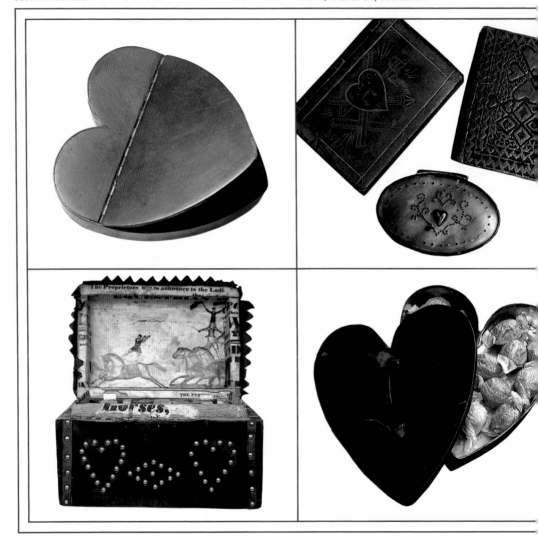

MINIATURE COVERED LEATHER BOX WITH BRASS-STUDDED
HEARTS. NEW ENGLAND. LATE 18TH CENTURY.

COVERED TIN BOX. VERMONT. LATE 19TH CENTURY.

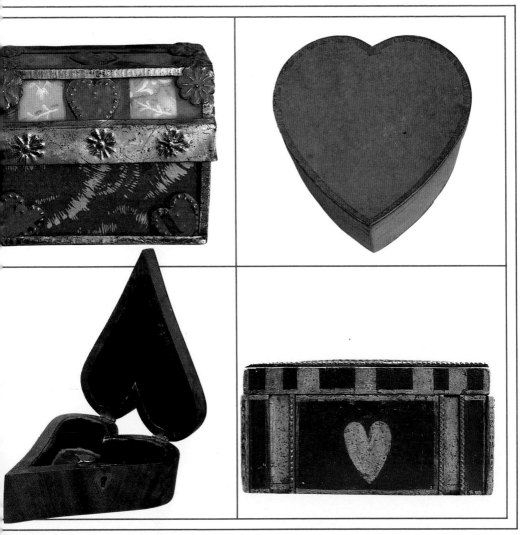

RED FOLK ART TIN BOX WITH TRAMP WORK AND
HEARTS. PENNSYLVANIA. LATE 19TH CENTURY.

VICTORIAN HATBOX COVERED WITH RED PAPER.

RED BOX WITH HEART-SHAPED KEY PLATE.
ENGLAND. C. 1830.

PAINTED BOX WEARS ITS ORIGINAL COAT OF MILK PAINT.
NEW ENGLAND. 18TH CENTURY.

HEART-DECORATED HORSE BRIDLE PIECES. C. 1900.

He hath a heart as sound as a bell,
and his tongue is the clapper;
for what his heart thinks his tongue speaks.

WILLIAM SHAKESPEARE

peak to his heart,
and the man becomes suddenly virtuous.

RALPH WALDO EMERSON

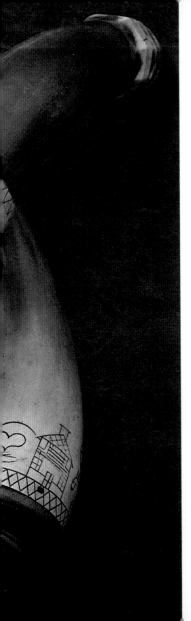

LEATHER CARD CASE WITH SILVER CORNERS AND HEART.
LEFT: POWDER HORNS WITH SCRIMSHAW. NANTUCKET. LATE 1700S.

rust thyself: every heart vibrates to that iron string.

RALPH WALDO EMERSON

MINIATURE BAND PAPER BOX USED FOR KEEPSAKES. PENNSYLVANIA. 18TH CENTURY.
RIGHT: STONEWARE CROCK. VERMONT. C. 1830.

BLUE-GRAY HEART ON HEART CHIP-CARVED STOOL. CONNECTICUT. EARLY 19TH CENTURY.

W

*e know the truth,
not only by the reason
but by the heart.*

BLAISE PASCAL

FOOTSTOOL, HEART INLAY DESIGN. VICTORIAN. C. 1880.

A

*good heart is better
than all the heads in the world.*

EDWARD BULWER-LYTTON

CLOCKWISE FROM TOP: WOOD AND PIERCED-TIN FOOT WARMER; CHILD-SIZE FOOT WARMER;
WOOL HOMESPUN BLANKET–PIN CUSHION WITH STITCHED HEART. EARLY 19TH CENTURY.

HEART ANDIRONS. NEW ENGLAND. LATE 18TH CENTURY. WOOD BELLOWS WITH CUT HEART DESIGN. EARLY 19TH CENTURY.

WIRE FIREPLACE FENDER. NEW ENGLAND. LATE 18TH CENTURY.

WOODEN HEART AND ARROW WEATHERVANE. PENNSYLVANIA. C. 1840.

I

shot an arrow into the air,
It fell to earth, I knew not where;
For so swiftly it flew, the sight
Could not follow it in its flight.

I breathed a song into the air,
It fell to earth, I knew not where;
For who has sight so keen and strong,
That it can follow the flight of song?

Long, long afterward, in an oak
I found the arrow, still unbroke;
and the song, from beginning to end,
I found again in the heart of a friend.

HENRY WADSWORTH LONGFELLOW

ACKNOWLEDGMENTS

Robert Kinnaman and Brian Ramaekers
Edwa Osborn
Rod Kiracofe
Gerri and Morgan MacWhinnie
Barbara Kaufman
Beverly Jacomini
Jeffrey Camp
George Weymouth
The Shelburne Museum
Bernard Berenholtz
Barbara Gray
Jane and George Harold
Paul and Dee Madden
Holly and Stephen Meier
Tom and Carolyn Porter
Sally Riffle
Marjorie Staufer
Dick and Sue Studebaker
Bob and Jackie Rose
The Winterthur Museum
Barbara Trujillo
Barbara Johnson
Patti Kenner
David Herrmann
Pam Reycraft
Everyone at Clarkson N. Potter

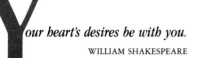

Your heart's desires be with you.

WILLIAM SHAKESPEARE

CRYSTAL WINEGLASS WITH ETCHED HEARTS AND BIRDS.
MASSACHUSETTS. LATE 19TH CENTURY.

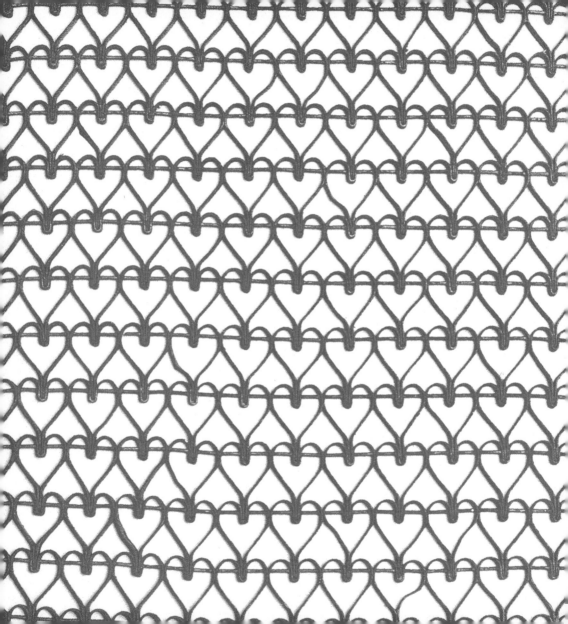